a glimpse of the rising sun

*to the ones who love deeply
and inevitably break hard.*

author's note

you can learn a lot in the span of a year.

i know i did.

this book is a collection of pieces i wrote in distinct stages of love and heartbreak: there's the beginning, the honeymoon phase when you first fall in love; there are the troubled waters, when your romanticization of it all is challenged and, of course, the gruelling heartbreak that follows when your suspicions are correct; but then, you come out in the end, knowing you'll find peace again.

this book is split into four parts that correspond with these stages, each named after a time of day. my hope is that you enjoy every piece as much as i enjoyed writing them.

preface

i'm well acquainted with the cycle of love.

it begins the moment you look at them from across the room, eyes glimmering with a sort of hope, anticipation, potential. it's the moment you hear their voice for the first time on the phone at midnight, voice hushed as to not be heard through the room's thin walls. the moment they begin to open up, begin to let you read their story and paint you a world that you swear is more colourful than anything you've ever seen. you breathe in, close your eyes, and feel the way the golden horizon embraces the end of the day. you aren't sure when a faint outline of their face replaced the usual darkness behind your eyelids, their smile nearly as bright as the sun's rays.

but right here, you feel safe.

you could stay here forever.

you feel like you've finally made it to the end of that treacherous trail you've been hiking for ages. you're right at the top of the mountain. you pitch the flag at the peak, hearing the way your cheers echo throughout the atmosphere. you look out below in awe of the journey, at each of the steep climbs and drops that almost made you turn around.

you're glad you didn't.

you reach your hands up towards the sky. now, there's someone there to grab hold of them. you feel something then: the folklore calls it butterflies, that warmth engulfing every limb that traces back to a nebula in your chest. when you hear them laugh, you hope the fluttering insects stay trapped beneath your rib cage until the end of time. you no longer dread the return to reality following sleep because, in the light of each new day ahead, you know they'll be full of love. it's something you don't think you'll ever get used to, but something you'll cherish as long as you can.

there's nothing like the reminder that you're worthy of all the things you convinced yourself you would never find in a world like this.
this is what they mean by things falling into place, by all the pieces coming together.

the emptiness is gone; you feel whole.

you can confidently say that everything is good.

although at some point, there's a shift. it's an unanticipated alteration of the trajectory of the story.

things feel displaced from the equilibrium that you thought you finally obtained, but you can't yet articulate what it all means. those hands are still within reach, your fingers fluttering in desperation to stay intertwined, but the grasp is not strong enough to keep you from losing your footing where you stand. your breath is shaky as you try to count each rapid beat of your heart: breathing in for 4, holding for 4, out for 6.

the butterflies' fragile wings fray at the edges. they feel much more like flies that buzz in your throat, making you forget how to swallow. the chaos leaves you wondering what could be going on beyond your immediate perceptions. you just *know* something is wrong, even when nothing has changed at first glance. to a passerby, it all looks the same. it's the most challenging item in the illustrated search-and-find.

but the reassurance you crave is not delivered as it once was. it feels like migraines and body aches before the

heavy rain and gloomy days set in. however, you don't
have a weatherman to tell you when this storm will pass.
it's like dusk falling upon you. it pushes you into an
insurmountable unconscious against your will.

you pinch yourself all over in hopes that you're simply in a
dream, that you'll wake up from this impending doom
where you're teetering on the edge. you feel like you're
about to lose it all. you just want the butterflies back, want
to revert to the beginning where you danced in the
sunshine under blue skies, inseparable from your lover.

now, you choke back the flies and pretend everything's
alright.

call it intuition, self-sabotage, an unfortunate pattern,
groundhog day—whichever string of words frames it
best—you know by now that you always end up here:
pacing within that ambiguous space between two small
towns.

it never is a dream, no matter how many desperate pleas
you send forth into the night. you try to think of the facts,
but all you know is that you were suddenly dropped off at

the side of the road. you're not too sure where you're headed anymore as the taillights disappear into the fog.

which way is home?

it's hard to tell when the one thing you called home has now left you dreamless in the dark.

the tears freeze on your cheeks, forming icebergs of lost potential and pain. you know your only option is to sleep. behind your swollen eyelids, you can still see that faint outline. but their bright smile has faded, and their final words echo in your ringing ears. you fix yourself a temporary bed of sorrow, holding yourself to keep warm.

it begins to consume you once you lay down.

you try to kick your way to the surface, though you're certain you'll drown right here where you are. you cry out curses on their name and sob along to the songs crickets play because, with your eyes closed, it feels like the embrace of the departed.

perhaps it would be easier to accept your fate, to stop trying to win the game when there's no more possible moves.

the night is long and void of light. it's spent breaking apart the puzzle you completed and trying to put it back together in hopes of comprehending all the lessons to be learned from what you've labelled in your mind as a tragedy. but you find that as you progress, there are pieces missing; you never did see the full image. there are things that make you realize that, even in the hurt, maybe there's a reason you ended up here.

maybe it wasn't such a tragedy after all.

it's with this epiphany that you catch a glimpse of the rising sun. the warm rays have been absent for so long that your frostbitten fingers burn in the light, turning the tips the colour of fiery passion. you notice the way the sun shines through the trees, stencilling abstract shapes into the dew-kissed grass. the pain in your hands begins to subside. though it may linger like a ghost at your bedside—barely enough to notice unless you were intently focused—you mean it this time when you tell the trees that you are okay. that, despite the events of the night prior, you feel strong enough to pull yourself up and stand with your thumb up at the side of the road as you trust your heart to bring you home.

you eventually appreciate the bumpy road. you allow anger to rise when it must, allow anger to recede when it must. you let your brows furrow and fists shake as you need. but you also understand that not all of the fault can be placed on someone else, not always.

so, you learn.

you welcome grief with open arms for the first time in your life rather than latch onto what was good until it suffocates. sometimes you cry, sometimes you scream, sometimes silence is all you need in the back of the car while the driver plays music in a language you don't speak. you feel, and feel, and feel.

although there's no feeling quite like finally pulling into the driveway of your safe place after all the pain you've endured alone. where the walls hug you dearly and the wood crackles in the fireplace, where the honey-sweetened tea steeps on the table and your bed is made. you wonder if it's a mirage of all you could ever wish for, if there's a chance you're still laying frozen on the forest floor from the night before.

but when you look out the window, you can still see that sun, the way it makes the sky so bright in contrast to the night.

you place your hand over your heart, feeling the way it tenderly beats.

yes, you are home.

part 1: embraces of a golden horizon

the talking stage

sing me songs to the tune of your favourite childhood memories; the ones that make your soft laugh echo in my ears much like the waves of the ocean in the broken shells i'd find on the beach as a kid.

unravel all the chaos in your mind with me. grant me permission to see your eyes glisten when you talk about your dreams and favourite things, and comfort you when your weary voice hesitates as you let all the obstacles that shaped your being drip from your tongue. let me read your story as though it were a world-renowned book sitting atop the highest shelf in my room.

i'll admit: i want to know your name inside-out, count the letters and rearrange them into anagrams to pass the time. i want to relish the flutter it gives me when it appears on my cracked screen each morning as you hope i've slept well.

i've grown to love the silence just as much as the playful banter that leaves a loud smile on my face.

sometimes, i wonder if you can hear the magnitude of it, or if perhaps the sound of yours is louder.

secrets

sit down
close our eyes
listen to the cicadas
how their harmonies crescendo
like orchestra strings
in the august sun.

set the scene of the climax of our story:
you pour the contents of your heart
onto the pavement
and it spells my name.

you say it's been
the hardest secret to keep
nearly breaking character
more times than fingers on your hands.

i laugh
and your face twists
in that way it does
whenever the pieces of a moment
don't quite fit together in your head.

it's my turn to spill my heart:
how funny is it that
it spells your name, too?

a glimpse of the rising sun

light

i watch you step out from behind the sun
and the chaos in my thoughts
unwinds into smooth streams
that make the pieces so much clearer
easier to fit together
as i solve the puzzle
of your alias:
you are the light i need
and you always have been.

you reach tenderly for my hand
and i lace my cold fingers into
the valleys of solace
i've craved
all my life
(and unknowingly had
right in front of me
all my life)
spending my time scrawling desperate essays
to persuade a make-believe audience that
they could feel just as much like home
as you've managed to
all the years i've known you.

and beneath the shade of the trees,
it's rather easy to conclude
that nothing compares
to the way you shine on me;
i know for certain that
it was always meant
to come back to you.

slow burn

baby, i don't care if we burn slow
let's bask in all the days
we spend waiting
for our flickering flame
to reach the quick
shelter it from the open window
wind blows
add some fuel every blue moon or two
keep the fire on its toes
we don't need to rush this love
let it take its time

long distance

the moon smiles when she sees us;
her saturated sky
the canopy under which we lie,
dreaming of a time
where we'll no longer rely
on intertwined voices
and invisible phone lines
to stitch our worlds together.

insomniac

you ask me why i'm still awake
and i laugh to myself
for how could you not know
it's because of you?

but i don't reveal
such inner-thinking
simply blame it on stress
and irregular circadian rhythms.

i quickly learn that
my poker face must be strong
when you sympathize with
my fictional insomnia.

you never were good
at seeing through me
but just this once,
i don't mind.

hold me

when my world is ablaze
the dark smoke closing its grip
while everything turns to dark ash,
it's you who i need.

hold me with all your might
until the sun reveals itself in my sky
and my lungs remember how to breathe
as all my jagged pieces come back together.

and as my eyelids fall heavy with sleep
in the earliest hours of the morning,
the sound of your hushed voice
reverberates endlessly in my head.
your amber eyes bring me to nirvana,
softened in that enchanting way
i have learned is reserved only for when
you say those three sweet syllables.

but my mind is cruel at this time of night;
your phantom touch lingers on my body
just long enough for me to question
the validity of its existence.
a mirage of your lips hangs above me,
its merciless taunting only
the preface of its journey towards
a destination to where it will never arrive.

i lie embraced within your fictitious presence,
my unconscious mind running wild
with relentless dreams about
when your arms will hold me next.

- can't wait to see you again

about you

they talk about love
rising in the night
crescent moon smiles
softening the shadows
that once cut deep

dark irises turned gold
rosy tunnel vision
with low aperture focus
to capture the subject
make them stand out
against the noise

wrapped up in velvet sheets
old records play lullabies
to lull the mind to sleep
it's okay if they skip
a beat or two

they talk about love
and i talk about you
how daisies grow
on the hill upon your nose

i rise for you
like the sun
send me to the stars
to the farthest galaxy
and i'd still find you
ambitions burning bright

i've never known you
any other way
caught in your gravity
voice like poetry
dissolve dark clouds
with every word you speak

i'll be in the audience
every single time
off-key notes
from comedy musicals
that float from lips
i'd kiss in this lifetime
and each one to follow

(taste my secrets
like vanilla custard
pretend you haven't
known them for years
and i'll pretend
the same of yours)

acne scars

you draw gentle lines across my face
connect the spots that
make me want to cover every mirror.

i tell you how my greatest wish
is to be given a smooth canvas
like the girls on tv
but you shake your head
and say each mark is like a star.

they turn my skin into
a series of constellations
as mesmerizing as the night sky.

i argue that i am nothing like the night sky
and would prefer to keep the stars up there
rather than allow them to take refuge on me
but have yet to find a remedy
despite searching for years.

(i am reminded constantly that
i need to do something about them).

but then you laugh
take my cheeks in your tender hands
and tell me i am the most beautiful thing
you have ever seen
and each spot on my face
only amplifies such a fact.

you kiss my forehead
and i could almost melt;
i think you are the only person to ever say
my stars are beautiful.

i want to cover the mirrors
a little less now.

when i knew

take my calloused hand
let's get lost in a reality
i can't fathom to be true
over the sand dunes
crashing down into you
teach me how to skip rocks
on the littered coastline
like we might've as kids
(the oldest trick;
i pretend i don't know it as
an excuse to hold my hips)
in the glow of the full moon
each stone plummets
much like my free-falling stomach
(i sigh through a smile
and say how bad i am at this,
you just hold me tighter)
i know right then
that i'm surely in love with you.

everything i wanted

i always loved the way
the sunlight that poured
from your amber eyes
was tinted a colour of rose
i had never encountered.

it enveloped me in a comfort
that hushed all my fears that
i was merely living in a dream
because somehow i had
everything i wanted
in you.

this is how you fall in love:

1. there's a pull, like the gentle tide drawn to the gleaming moon. it's too early to understand why, but you know that you want so badly to wrap yourself in the pages of their story. you'll want to brush the dust off and immerse yourself in each letter even if it's written like a shakespearean tragedy.

2. they'll read you short excerpts if you play your cards right. you'll abandon sleep to listen because restfulness became second-best in your mind from the moment they first spoke your name. now you'll look for any opportunity to hear their voice, even if for a second, for there's no sound quite like it.

3. you'll begin to see the colour of their eyes in the sky. you'll see their face in the garden stones because they had a rock collection as a kid and the ones that sparkled were their favourite. see them in the produce aisle because they once ate so many grapes as a dare that they now get sick just looking at them. in the song they said was the greatest of

all time (you'll listen to it thirty-six times in one day even though it's not at all your taste).

4. they'll save you a seat when you walk in late with two coffees instead of one. in a crowded place, you'll somehow know exactly where they'll be. when you have to part, when you find yourselves on opposite ends of the room, you'll somehow gravitate back to the centre, back together. it's a phenomenon for which you'll never have a name.

5. you'll want to walk with them through trenches, when explosions threaten to tear it all apart. you'll want to be there when they're on the verge of breaking and sit with them in the silence for as long as they need you to. you know it won't always be soaring hand-in-hand above the clouds. you won't care. you'll want to witness the rises and falls, and you know you'll stay for both.

6. you'll feel whole on your own, of course. but the joy when you're tucked under their arm, listening to the rain drum inconsistent rhythms on the window is unmatched. they'll tenderly trace your skin with all the hurdles and the obstacles, the

butterflies and things-gone-right. and as they do
so, you'll piece it all together and realize: *this is
how you fall in love.*

part 2: as dusk falls upon me

speed dial

i know it's your number
my phone dials
when i press 2
but i no longer recognize
the voice on the other end
of the line

a glimpse of the rising sun

foundation

there's a moment where
the blushing veil you've spent
months sewing by hand
is torn from your grasp,
sending you straight into
the forest fire
in desperation to
recover it.

but your heart will sink
into the well of tears
yet to be cried
as the flames melt your convictions
until the cracks you've patched
with plasticine
begin to show
and all you've come to know
crumbles to the earth.

nothing's pretty
without the filter of your love
brightening the edges
to look like a dream.

but the picture is clearer
when the aperture is high
and you realize that
band-aids can't fix
a fragile foundation.

it was doomed from the start.

trust

i part my lips to speak
but i've forgotten how to make a sound
since your grand ricochet,
where you took my trust with you
on the way out.

i have spent every gruelling second since
trying to understand why we're here.

i know the map makes sense
from your point of view
and i pretend it does from mine too
even if the colour-codes and crossroads
drop my soul into
the gutters below street level
just to mollify the guilt you hold from
coaxing me into your familiar arms
only to back away
as soon as you had my head
on a golden plate.

my bodyguards have yet to disarm
so i take the long way home
because i know that
if i think about it too much
one of them may fire at you
(although sometimes
i wish one would;
i only said it was okay
to make you feel better).

i cannot imagine losing you
but i have not rebuilt enough of my walls
to bear your presence just yet
and if i'm honest,
i don't know how long it will take.

so where do we go from here
now that we can't deny
that things have changed
from how they used to be?

a glimpse of the rising sun

i'd bow at your feet
and leave not an inch of skin untouched by my lips
if i knew it would anchor you to me
you are not really here
just going through motions
as the hot wax drips and sears my blistered hands
you look but don't see
i'd burn forests for you
collect the remains to reignite the flame
(we could start over like that, don't you think?)
you ask why the fire's burning so hard
pick the wax from my palms
but not tenderly
hardened heart falling on the floor
you have more important things to do
move like you're in a hurry
don't meet my eyes
so i count the lines in your forehead
it's the next best thing

- *you are not really here*

i have to heal
from two heartbreaks instead of one
because the contract
needs you to agree to pick up
where he left off
and show me all the ways
i crave to be loved
to convince me that i am worth something,
that i am not just another in a line up.

i thought i was clever each time
i slid the page across the table,
three attempts to splash ink on the signature line
even though i knew deep down
you wouldn't be the right person for the job.

but i had already bonded to your laugh
the way your stories soothed my soul,
and i did not want to let it all go
despite how badly it was hurting me
and how badly i was hurting you
by refusing to amend the fine print
that never considered your own requisites.

a glimpse of the rising sun

so i have to heal
from two heartbreaks instead of one
because you knew when it was time to part
while i was too focused on
how to make things work
exactly the way i wanted,
the way i wished things
would have been with him.

i know i've earned it,
the guilt i feel each time i think of you,
though you're too nice to agree
or accept my apology.

and that's the part that hurts the most.

- if you're reading this, know that you deserve better

ruin me

oh, would i ever let you ruin me
again and again

tear me open without sedation and
stitch me back together
just pick at the thread
until it frays and
you have to sew me
once more

because i'd rather have you close—
even if it means
running my fingers
haphazardly through your hair
as you chew on my heart—
than watch you walk away
without turning back
leaving me with nothing but
the remnants of you
in the words i write

a glimpse of the rising sun

runaways

run away with me tonight.

let's kiss all the lights
that line the boulevard
of the main street
in our small town
after every tenth one
you can turn and press
your lips to mine.

you'll say it's your way
of keeping count
that it's easiest to count up by tens
but you've never been good at telling lies.

my syncopated heartbeat
will spell out "i love you"
in morse code
i'll let you feel it if you ask
broadcast it over the loudspeakers
at the gravel baseball diamond
behind the catholic school
we attended as kids

how nice it would be to
give the people sweet music
to fall asleep to
give them a taste of how it feels
to love you.

then you'll take my hand
and waltz us around the bases
say that you hit a home run
when you met me.

we can take your car and drive
until there's no more road to cover
buy cheap liquor to celebrate
kick off our shoes at an old motel
a toast to forever.

we'll take silly photos
with disposable cameras we find
at a convenience store
with lighting that makes
everything look blue
and eat the film when we get hungry
it'll keep the memories safe inside
losing them would be a shame.

a glimpse of the rising sun

(so would losing you).

so before you tell me with regret
that we've come to a crossroads
and you don't think you can stay anymore
(i know it's what you've been thinking about)
what if we run away
even if it's only for tonight?

you can leave in the morning
if i fail to change your mind.

the day you left

in my eyes
you died two times:

the first being when
you didn't turn back
to wave in that shy way
that made you look
so much like a child
(but maybe not as innocent)

the second was realizing
i'd probably never see you again
as we exited stage right
without making eye contact
(we didn't even bow
at the end of our act?)
and somehow
that hurt more
than the day you left

hide and seek

you told me to close my eyes
turn around and count to five
underneath the oak tree
while you ventured off to
your best hiding spot.

you said it would be fun—
i thought so too;
i was good at this game
when i was little—
kissed my forehead
and told me
you'd see me soon.

but now i'm not so sure
where to go
because i've been searching
for longer than i can track
covered every inch of my map
and still can't seem to find you
anywhere.

casiah cagan

just the same

i noticed that i try to look for you
in every person i fall in love with
and convince myself that
their heart resembles yours.

but none of them
ever live up to you
no matter how many
similarities
i try to find.

in the end,
i am always disappointed
get my heart broken
(stupid me)
but i liked to imagine
it would be different with you
if i ever got that chance.

but my imagination was just that;
i must not have known you
as well as i thought
for you broke me just the same.

won't you dance with me?

i've memorized the waltz of unrequited love:
each note of the melody,
those false steps against the beat,
the moment bows drop from strings
when my confession is met with silence.
i've become acquainted with
the way each one pursues their exits—
i like to note the subtle differences
as they grow further out of sight—
before the conductor raises his baton
and the orchestra begins from the top
inviting the next contestant in
to dance with me.

when i say i like to see the good in people,
i mean that i like to see their potential
because i love how his voice
sounds like the exact shade of rose
in which i view my world.

i say my perfect place is perfect
just because i can picture him there
more clearly than anything.

but it's not really him; it never was.

i give too much
and expect too much
and ignore each time he admits
he could never do any of it for me.

but i keep persisting because
the image of what could be looks so sweet
if only he could see what i see.

he often tells me i am sweet.

and each time he does
i am reassured that we're okay

despite the rainy soundscape
that i play as i fall asleep
saying otherwise.

i like to think that everything is okay.

but when i live in memories
yet to be created
i lose sight of the present
the truth lies fay beyond
my narrow line of vision
and it only seems to come into view
when he asks if we can talk.

- i didn't hear the music stop

casiah cagan

permanent

sometimes,
when i can't sleep,
i like to direct
parallel timelines
building a vision
of all the ways
you and i could exist

do exist

have existed

in every universe.

but even when i
have control
over each facet
of the story,
i can't seem to
write an ending
that does not involve
your packed bags
fidgeting hands

figure in the doorway
getting ready to leave
and i wonder if
part of me always knew
you weren't meant
to be permanent

deja vu

i got my heart broken
nearly 6 months to the day
its delicate shards first glistened
on my bedroom floor

it felt a lot like deja vu
when the pieces slid across
the cherry laminate
in the middle of a
sunny afternoon
and i almost admired
the way they caught the light

even when bracing for impact
the paralysis was inevitable
when i realized i'd never
hear his voice again
at 11:23 pm

i've never loved anything
quite like i did his laugh
and his voice was the only thing
that could lull me to rest

back when my body
forgot the recipe for sleep

i wish i could have called
one last time
and listen to him excitedly recount
plotlines of shows
i'll never watch
wonder about the future
complain about the little things
before my phone rang
on a sunny afternoon

i got my heart broken again
nearly 6 months to the day
but the difference was that back then
the scratchy carpet
was good at keeping
all the pieces in the place
even if i was still picking out bits
so many months later
feet freckled with fresh cuts
that never seemed to heal

i could still feel the way
he'd gently twirl my curls
around his finger
and periodically pull me closer
as we'd lay and watch tv

i could never admit that
i etched his image into every wall
because i was scared
i'd forget what he looked like
when i didn't hear from him
for two weeks

he couldn't look me in the eye
when he came back

i laid on his side of the bed
and muffled my cries with pillows
until they stopped smelling like him

i got my heart broken again
nearly 6 months to the day
but there was no difference
not really
as much as i try to look for one

the similarities were
hidden in plain sight
merely shades of the same colour

but acknowledging their relation
would mean that
there were still shards
sitting in the carpet
that belonged to someone else
to someone i could only have vicariously

so why was i surprised
when things ended the same way
when it all pointed to a similar fate
from the beginning?

dinner guests

somehow
i always end up back here:
my thoughts ricochet off of
wasted potential
that hangs me to dry
in my nicest dress
while the clouds
hold back tears
another tally to add
to the stone wall
an ode to those
who came for dinner
but departed before
the main course.

i decided that
maybe it's best if
i stop setting two plates at the table;
absences are much less noticeable
when you're only
seating one.

a glimpse of the rising sun

or maybe i should simply
stop answering the door
when they come knocking;
if you don't invite the guests inside,
if you don't run to the window,
it's easier to pretend
that no one is home.

i do not need to endure the leaving
if i do not expect anyone to stay.

part 3: dreamless in the dark

punchline

they say it's funny the way things turn out sometimes.

i suppose it's true;

your departure was the perfect punchline.

october

you were
october;
a golden embrace shielding me from the crisp air
that turns my fingertips a numbing white,
freezing their hold on the fears
that wake me beneath the moonlight.

i've never liked new beginnings
but i especially despise
the melodramatic descent of leaves
and the extinguished vibrancy of the world
that comes at the cusp of endings.

i thrive in constants
but the consistency i crave
cannot be found in the seasons,
for even october turns to december
and your memory is not enough
to keep me warm through the winter.

north star

do you know that i talk to the sky about you? i've been telling it about you for months. i wonder if it can picture you each time i come to it with a new memory to add to a bank of hazy imagery.

when i first open the window, i whisper your name as though to preface a sacred ritual. i want the clouds to learn it and keep it safe so the world never forgets you.

sometimes, i wonder if they've begun to fall in love with it like i fell in love with you.

but i hope they don't fall as hard as i did, for i know they're just as delicate as i am. they would have crumbled when i opened the window that one night and your name did not follow. i had already crumbled; what a mess it would have been if the clouds did too.

since then, i have written prayers to the navy skies and begged the stars that live there to detail why we were fated to break when the signs that brushed a golden glow upon the woodsy trails pointed to you being all that i looked for.

even before i gave my mind permission to label the
epiphany as such, i always knew you to be unparalleled in
as many ways as there are stars in that sky that i talk to
about you.

i ask if there's a chance that you were the one; it always
felt like you were the one.

but the pit in my stomach counteracts: would we now be
driving through this inescapable ghost town at the border
of all that used to be—a place of warm comfort now
observable only through a sliver in the iron wall which
keeps us out— if you truly were my north star?

i have been listening intently for weeks now, but the sky
has fallen silent. it has yet to provide a verdict.

i pretend i don't already know it.

safe

my room is dark
curtains drawn
i'm missing the way
your lips would
gently find my forehead
your arms holding me near
as if to say
"you're safe
here"

i was
and i wish
it lasted
longer

reality

i am shackled to a version of you that lives
within the constraints of my tumultuous mind.

she has yet to understand that these thoughts
are now fictional fairy tales from the past.

they are no longer reality,
if they ever even were.

each night, she searches tirelessly
for all the light i saw in you
and excitedly plays compilations
of her found treasures
on the white walls of my bedroom
in hopes they bring me the joy they always did
before i allowed sleep to take me to my dreams.

i don't have the heart to tell her to stop,
for it would break her to know that her work
is only casting me farther into the shadows
and worsening wounds she doesn't know exist.

so i smile and thank her profusely
as i usually do before i close my eyes,
hoping that tomorrow
will be the first of those absent of you.

i am still hoping.

linear

they say healing is not linear.

i know it all too well, but do i ever wish it were.

how powerful it would be to accurately predict
the way each night unfolds
and brace for the accompanying pain.

at least then, i would know the next day

and the next day

and the next

would be better

as i'd gradually learn to be okay without you.

because i never know if tomorrow brings
a plummet from the peak i've conquered

(lately, it seems to)

how do you brace for impact
when the ground collapses under your feet
and your scarred hands are too tired
to continue hanging on?

ashes

i watch your ashes settle
onto the floor
from where i lay in my bed

i haven't moved in days

they fall with the delicacy of snowflakes
despite their inherent heaviness

like clockwork, i force myself up
and sweep them into neat little piles

i always ensure there are seven

one
two
three
four
five
six
seven

one pile for each month

casiah cagan

i count seven times to check

i observe my work
through a thin veil of saltwater
and pray that this is the last time
but then the wind blows my window open
and your remnants are lifted back into the air
where they swirl around like a hurricane
and leave me begging for truces
i'll never be granted

i crawl back into bed
and shield myself with lavender covers
while i wait for your ashes to settle
so i can do it all again

i hold an image of you in my head. it just sits there, an etch-a-sketch that doesn't disintegrate like the instructions say it should when i throw my head against the wall in my room routinely upon the hour.

i've got a bruise that's turned my favourite shade of purple above my right eyebrow.

i tell myself that it means i'm one step closer to not thinking about you like that anymore.

but i don't know if i'm getting any closer because there you are, an image in my head that looks as happy as you did the last time i saw you.

we were driving down the freeway in the morning light. i pretended i didn't notice the way you were staring at me from your place in the passenger seat, the corners of your lips slightly upturned in drunken admiration, back when we both thought about each other like that.

but now i talk to the image of you in my head because i haven't heard from you in a few weeks and it's getting strange. i'm starting to hate the way the you in my mind responds exactly the way i want.

i've never known the you in real life to do such a thing;
you were always good at grounding me, at being reckless
and unpredictable and spontaneous. the opposite of me.

it's why i liked you so much.

why i still like you so much.

so hearing you say all the things i want to hear is starting
to get old. it's starting to get strange.

my father stands in my doorway and asks how you are, a
routine much like my head's calculated connections with
my bedroom wall. he asks often because he knows we're
best friends. or rather, he thinks we're best friends; i get
the feeling that we've been demoted from that place.
but when my father asks how you are, he doesn't know
this. i haven't told him that i haven't heard from you in a
few weeks and it's probably because i still think about you
like that and you might still think about me like that.

so for the first time since i met you, for these past few
weeks in this weird in-between, i don't have a damn clue
how you are. i lie and say you're doing well, that you
finally quit your job and you fixed the brakes in your car

and your mom is getting better even though i don't know if
any of these are true.

but it must be convincing because my dad nods and asks
me to tell you he says hi.

i tell him i will.

he doesn't know that this is a lie, either.

i hate that i don't know how you are; i almost always know
the answer because you are so brutally truthful when i ask
("it's been rough") ("en route to rock bottom") ("i've had
better times"). i feel like if i asked you now, you wouldn't
be that honest ("i'm good") ("i'm fine") ("doing alright").
but since i haven't talked to you in a few weeks, and we're
both too stubborn to break that streak, i'll never be able to
test my theory.

maybe once we both stop thinking about each other like
that, we can forget about all of this and go back to the way
things were.

so all i can do now is sulk on my bed and press the bruise
on my forehead to remind me that i need to stop thinking

about you like that. it brings me to tears sometimes, but i have no choice because when i look in the mirror, the bruise opens its mouth and tells me that there is no coming back from this, no going back to the way things were no matter how many veins i pop wishing so hard that we could.

that's when i press into it harder, trying to get it to shut up. i don't like what it tells me. i don't know how to tell you that i want to go back to the way things were, but i don't want to stop thinking about you like that because i've never been more sure of anything than i am of you. though this makes me wonder if maybe the bruise is right, if maybe we'll always be stuck in this place because i can't stop thinking about you like that.

have you stopped thinking about me like that?

- words that are better left unsaid

drowning in you

i used to think that
the most painful part of healing was
that first lonesome week
where insomnia ruled my nights
and the persistent whispers
that told me i was inadequate
because i couldn't made you happy
sounded a lot like you.

i thought it was the unwelcome memories
playing endlessly behind my eyelids
like a broken film reel.

no matter how hard i pressed
my palms into them,
they refused to go away.

or maybe even the way
i had to painfully remind myself each day
that the only person i cared to speak to
was the last person who
craved my company.

but i've learned that it's none of these.

it's when days pass and finally
my smile is no longer a mask
for eyes swollen with perpetual sorrow;
my body no longer aches
in all the places void of your touch;
my heart no longer
cries out for you in my darkest hours.

it's then,
when i think i might be okay again,
that a forceful wave of despair
suddenly drowns me
in my favourite images of you.

while i struggle to stay afloat
in these roaring waters,
arms flailing in desperation to
find something to hold
to get me through the storm,
your outreached phantom hand
ruthlessly reminds me
that you are not here
to rescue me.

rock bottom

standing in frigid waters,
i walk with the remnants of my poise
out to where my feet can no longer touch
and sink into the suffocating realization
that you were never quite what i thought.

i get angry at the sea
for playing such wicked games with my trust.
he fills my lungs with sharp liquid
that freezes my limbs in place
and dares to tell me i am hyperbolizing fiction.

i want nothing more than to perform
elaborate dances of my fury
and make it known how much hurt
has seeped into every bone in my body
at his mercy.

but instead, i apologize
and ask for a second chance
because i don't like the disdain in the voice
of the entity who once promised
i'd never end up here.

when i'm met with silence,
i look up to the moon for comfort
and smile at the way she encapsulates
all of the beauty of the sea
that i have always adored.

even though i can hear
the echoes of my slowing heartbeat
as my frail body continues to sink,
i bask in the comfort of the water's embrace
for it's one thing i've missed dearly.

the shimmering light at the surface
makes for a pretty image of what could be.
it distracts me from the danger
that surrounds me
from where i cling to you at rock bottom.

a glimpse of the rising sun

you told me you missed me yesterday,
but you didn't mean it in the way
plants on dusty shelves
crave the sun when
the blinds stay closed for a few days.

they begin to shrivel
in the absence of their lifeline.

that's how i miss you.

but when you told me you missed me yesterday,
it felt more like you meant it in the way
a pretty flame longs for a wick
to keep it burning bold and bright.

the wick has lots to give,
and the flame has lots to take.

so when you told me you missed me yesterday,
i had to ignore it
and skip to the part
where i ask you how you are
because my ribcage contracted
in that way it does

when i glance at my phone
and see it light up with a notification from you.

but you don't miss me like that.

- "i miss you" means different things to us

lookalike

i put down my drink and all the boys turn around as if the crash of the glass against the table was a call specific to them. i'm not used to all-eyes-on-me, but i take it as an opportunity to try to paste your face onto theirs to see who matches best.

when they've taken a good look at me, decide i'm not quite worth it and return to their nonsensical conversations, i realize it's significantly easier to assign you to the backs of their heads. it's too easy to tell when his eyes aren't that same mix of jade and gold and his nose isn't crooked on the bridge. but when i see the backs of their heads, it's easier. one more drink and it'll be even more so.

i can make one of them look like you if i try hard enough.

i can turn him into you if i try hard enough.

i pick one out from the crowd who's already got your curly hair. i let that satisfy the requirements i've carved in my mind.

he's not really like you in any other way, not in the
slightest. not by looking at the back of his head, anyway.
i'm sure he doesn't have your sly smile, your dad jokes,
your gentle touch. i pretend it's good enough; i have to be
okay with good enough just as i have to be okay with
knowing that i can't have you despite wanting nothing
more.

asphalt

i carved your name into the fresh asphalt on the road beside the crumbling curb a few months ago.

i had to stop walking that way because my chest implodes when the letters catch my eye under the streetlights and my throat burns from the chokehold of your ghost. you're immortalized in the space where my thoughts of you are no longer sprinkled along the sidewalk, so others still have a chance to wonder about you.

i've learned to tie those thoughts tightly now that i go the other way (i don't want to litter blue memories across the manicured lawns of miserable people) but sometimes they still slip out. i have to scramble to retrieve them before the passersby watch me fall apart. they'd have to step over me like they might a broken vase of dead roses as i'd find consolation in the cracks in the concrete.

but i never fully fall apart; i patch myself up with band-aids and smile at the passersby. i ask them how they are and they ask me how i am and i tell them i am doing good because how would they know that it's not true?

when it gets too warm and my body is on fire, i turn
around and retrace my steps so i don't encounter your
name in the asphalt.

and like the curb beside it, i let myself crumble once i've
reached home and tear the band-aids off.

holding space

i don't think you know just how much space i've been
holding for you all this time.

i hold space in all the places where my friends try to tell
me that there's not a single drop of fault in my veins;
where my therapist says the solutions to my hurt hide;
during the weeks i was embarrassed to weep in front of my
mother because i couldn't conjure a single word that didn't
taste like you; in the places where every word i write is
tied to.

no matter how long someone is gone, i am the type of
person who will continue to hold space for them.

just in case they come back.

because wouldn't it be funny if they did?

i often allow my mind to wander to the smoothness of your
cheeks, the way the shape of your eyebrows made your
face look so kind and youthful, how brightly your smile
shone in the darkness of my bedroom.

i wonder how you're doing, if your brother passed his policing exam, if your aunt has been well, if you did decide to start seeing your dad more often.

i wonder if you found these past few months as difficult as i have.

were you grieving too?

it would make me feel less bad about the hell i've been going through.

i hold space for you even on the days where the creeks carved in my cheeks burn like the hot sun on our backs with your hand in mine. i wish i could open my window and scream my hatred for you until my lungs are fatigued from fury and every resident of my small town knows your name. they'll draw your picture for the blacklist and meet you at the border of nowhere should you try to enter.

but sometimes, i want you to enter. i want you to come to my house and ring the doorbell and tell me how wrong you were to walk away the way you did. i want you to bring me out onto the patchy grass in my front yard and dance

with me beneath that towering oak tree that should have
been cut down decades ago.

but i'll take a chance with danger if it means we'll meet
there. we can dance to "try" by blue rodeo because i
dreamed we danced along to that song the night you kissed
me for the first time. i've wanted to dance to it with you
ever since.

i never told you, but i wish i did. maybe then, we would
have gotten the chance.

so, if you came back, i would want to play it so loud for all
the neighbours to hear, and we could drown out their calls
and shaking fists with our laughter. i would dance with you
even if the sky was sobbing and we sank in the mud as
you'd twirl me around and whisper how sorry you were
and how you would do anything to have the privilege to
welcome me into your life again.

i hold space for you because even though i know such a
scenario is fictional, even though i know part of me would
be livid if it came true, another part of me dies each day it
doesn't.

birthday

there is a nook in my body
that stores all the aging archives
attempting to preserve your memory.

you've now lived
in my imagination
for a longer number of days
than you lived in my reality.

i wake up each morning
to a voice in my head
reading your biography aloud.

i've never memorized a story
like i have yours
but i don't know what to do
with all the pages
now that i have no one
to recite the words to.

a glimpse of the rising sun

today is your birthday.

(i wonder if you still remember mine)

i hope it's a happy one.

i wish i could reach out and tell you this
because maybe then,
it would dull the ache born from
the unsettling revelation that
i'll have to remember you
for far longer than i ever knew you.

destination

i saw nine cars that looked like yours today
while driving on the freeway.

i was travelling along the same route
i would have taken to your house
not all that long ago
yet for the first time
you were not the destination.

it hated it.

i saw nine cars that looked like yours today
and i entertained the idea
that each one i saw meant
you were thinking of me right then.

i tallied them in my head:
onetwothreefour
cross to make five
sixseveneightnine.

a glimpse of the rising sun

my knuckles kept count too,
morphing into miniature white mountains
around the steering wheel
one by one.

every tooth in my clenched jaw
shattered under pressure
the cracks and pops increasing
with every exit i passed.

i couldn't bring myself
to spit all the pieces out
though they were as sharp as
your voice the last time you talked to me.

i saw nine cars that looked like yours today,
although only two of them were the same colour.

i entertained the idea
that one of them was you.

REM

i dreamt of you last night;
it's been months since i've last been
graced by your presence
always unwelcome in my subconscious
but notorious for finding ways
to unexpectedly weave itself into me.

so i was not surprised when
an REM version of you
called me in the middle of the afternoon
on a tuesday
(it wasn't really tuesday
but it felt like a tuesday to me
time is strange in dreams).

i didn't know who was calling
but i answered the phone
like it was my best friend
and even the lifeless version of me
lying in her bed
felt her heart implode
when my ear filled with
the sound of my nickname

spoken as though it were wrapped
in the most luxurious velvet.

it's been nearly a year
since i heard your voice last
but it's one of those things
i could recognize anywhere
no matter how much time has lapsed.

so undoubtedly you.

but, you see, it was not really you
because it was not really you telling me how
you had been thinking too much about me
since you left me standing in my doorway
on a rainy autumn afternoon
with the glass of water from which you drank
as you fumbled your final words to me
still sitting on the counter.

somehow, we ended up in the place
that you swore we never would
but i've learned that
promises are too fragile
to not be broken

even at the hands of someone
who made you believe
in forever.

you called me on that tuesday afternoon
and asked for my forgiveness
for the treacherous journey you led me on
before abandoning me in unknown territory,
for all the ways you wished
you had done better
and all the ways you wished
to show me you can.

but, you see, it was not really you;
it was a carefully crafted film i often go to see
on the nights when
your phantom hand leaves a heavy residue
between our falsely intertwined fingers.
it shows me what it would look like
if our paths crossed once again
(i may not be a professional critic
but i'd give it 5 stars).

i'd go take down the battered "wanted" posters
and reverse your eternal banishment

so you could drive to my house
like you used to every week last summer
we'd laugh and label it one big misunderstanding
and you'd hold me for as many days
as you'd been away.

i memorized the script
like i did my times tables as a child;
i've never tasted something so sweet.

so i was almost angry
when i went off-course
(but, you see, it wasn't really me)
and threw all my fury at you through the phone
for having such audacity to ask for pity
when you dragged me across all the glass
you shattered during your exit
because you wanted the script to be written
exclusively from your point of view.

but you failed to realize
that it was from your point of view the whole time
and when i finally regained my voice,
you never bothered to read it from mine.

don't you know that
i abandoned myself in search of your soul
and even 8 months after you,
i still have yet to find her?

they say to forgive is to have courage
so call me a coward when i say
forgiveness was one thing
i will never give to you.

i hung up the phone
before i could comprehend your words
before i could be punished by a harsh reply
or seduced by a sweet one.

and that's when i woke up
in my bed at home
disappointed that i left,
wishing i would have stayed just a bit longer
to hear your voice
even if it wasn't quite yours.

i don't love you anymore, but i still remember how to get to your house.

i could do it now if i tried; i could get in my car and shift my mind into autopilot and let it guide me all the way to you, even though it's been months since i last did.

i miss the way your face lit up when you saw me waiting for you whenever i'd pick you up, your smile brighter than anything i've ever seen as you'd tell me how happy you were to see me.

you had such a goofy smile.

it was one of the things i loved most about you.

the drive to you would take me 53 minutes (i know it's because i drive a little too fast).

i memorized every turn and every merge just as easily as i did the way home as a kid (and in a way, driving to you was once the way home). i know all the detours on the back roads and i know how to get there from my old apartment, too.

i moved out back in the winter.

you don't know that.

i wonder if you think i still live there.

when i'd drop you off at home after the sun had gone down, i would never drive away until i saw you walk around the corner, beyond the radius of the streetlamp's glow.

that was my way of figuring you were safe.

you probably don't know that either.

i don't love you anymore but the thought of ever seeing you again leaves me immobilized with fear. sometimes i wonder if you think about what would happen if you ever saw me again, if you're just as scared as i am because of what you did. if you're scared because maybe you don't love me anymore, but sometimes you miss my lopsided smile or soft voice or the way no one ever put you first like i did. maybe you're scared because you know that no one will ever love you like i did.

you're scared to be confronted by what you lost.

no, i don't love you anymore, but i think about you more often than i'd like to admit. i think a lot about the time we spent together, the good more than the bad, and i can't tell if i like it that way.

i don't love you anymore, but i wouldn't mind if you told me you wanted to try again. that you want to see my car in the parking lot, want to re-learn the handshake you crafted with my brother, want me to read to you and play with your hair while you lay your head in my lap, want to walk aimlessly through the grocery store aisles, want to listen to me sing to you, want to pretend you understand all the complex thoughts that run through my mind, that you want to take my hand and promise to not let go.

but i would be a fool to wish upon the stars every night to be granted this. so instead, i'll walk around with the weight of these memories that i don't have the courage to discard quite yet.

i know i'll be forced to clutch my limbs and console them when i do see you again. i wonder if you'll be doing the same.

i don't love you anymore, but i hope it'll be a while before that time comes.

i'm not ready.

- *an email sitting in my drafts*

after all this time

my lips are cracking
from passing my tongue over them
trying to mimic the way
you did it when you'd kiss me.

it didn't taste like copper then, though.

even in june i catch myself shivering;
you were always warm enough for the both of us
and i have yet to successfully
replicate the feeling.

i break out in cold sweats
under the skyscraper i've built with
weighted blankets.

you've been more present lately,
memories of you surfacing much too easily
despite convincing my soul months ago
that i locked every last one in the vault.

i must have forgotten
to turn the key.

sometimes i smile at them;
sometimes i like to pretend
i'm living in those moments
with you again.

but even the joy cannot drown
the pain of knowing that
part of me still loves you
after all this time.

a glimpse of the rising sun

i heard a voice today
that sounded too much like yours
coming from a few tables over
in the study hall

i thought it was you
such uncanny resemblance
but i refused to look
clutched my sanity so hard
my hands shook

i swore i could have died right there
in the middle of the crowded room

- i think i still miss you.

dreaming

yesterday,
i met you at the place
where my dreams touch
the light of dawn.

i've been seeing you there
quite often lately
and i wish i knew why.

i confess,
i would have once preferred
to burn
than see you,
for you were only ever interested
in disguising chaos
as the one thing i love most.

you know you are my weakness;
you never come to me in peace.

but for the first time—
yesterday—
you embodied serenity.

a glimpse of the rising sun

and for the first time—
yesterday—
i didn't fight immersion in your eyes
or be quick to tell you off.

i let myself be loved by you,
even if it was only for pretend.

you came over
kissed me at the door
like you always used to
we laughed as we descended the stairs
said that everything was fine
and erased our broken hearts
from the sands of time
though part of me still knew
you had been gone
for much too long.

i was hesitant to let you hold me again
pretending i wasn't shouldering
discomfort in your presence
(i'm not very good at pretending).

you wrapped your arms around me then
laying beside me on the couch
and buried your head in my neck.

i instantly melted into your touch.

i finally felt like i was home again.

i hadn't felt at home since you left.

i told you this,
told you that i missed you,
that i thought i didn't anymore
but i undeniably do.

you told me you missed me too.

i could have stayed there forever.

for the first time—
yesterday—
i was upset to wake up and find
that i could no longer feel the way
your whole body moves when you laugh.

where i'd once rue sleep
out if fear you'd meet me there,
i almost look forward to it.

it's my only opportunity to see you now
even if it's only for pretend.

part 4: a glimpse of the rising sun

us in hindsight

i stab my sharpest pins into
the maddening dissonance between
my words and sly movements,
the lists of unattainable expectations
that read like never-ending to-do lists,
the way i made you liable
for each ounce of my happiness.

all the points are connected
with the chain of the ruby pendant
you gave me for my birthday
(white gold was never my colour).

it spells out an apology across my wall
that i know you will never see
for writing you as the antagonist of the story
when i was just as guilty.

bleed for you

you come crawling back
on bruised hands and knees
equipped with a victimized apology
assuming that i still bleed for you
clouded gaze, red paths drip onto the snow
hoping you'd follow me home
while you were quick to sever
the frayed string of dull gold
and made sure i watched you go.

so you do not get to materialize
and act as though you can still read my mind
because you are the last person
to whom i'd give that right.

and surely, you must not know
(if you did, you wouldn't be at my door):
i don't bleed for anyone
and i certainly don't
bleed for you anymore.

gardens of babylon

try as you might to forget,
i know you are preoccupied with
gold-tinged memories of
my sun-kissed curls,
spending these cold nights
etching your attempts
to solve the complex mystery
of who i could have possibly been
into your lonely ceiling.

but even then,
you can only theorize my existence
for i am the gardens of babylon;
i stand with my head in the clouds
and humble you
with my ethereal beauty.

i give you a glimpse into
your most perfect image of paradise
and give you all you could ever wish for
each time you step
into my sacred embrace.

but now i'll disappear from you without a trace
and leave you wondering
how much of me was all in your head
as you desperately try to piece together
the words others write about me
attempting to rebuild my body
in the way you last remember it.

but you'll eventually realize
that in all of history,
you'll never encounter
another like me.

immortalized

i know you must wish
you never got a poet alone
wish you could erase
the day my lips explained
that i hold the power to both
love you
and destroy you
in as many ways as i can reconfigure
the english alphabet
into metaphors and hyperboles.

you signed across the dotted line
with your tongue
thinking that i'd never have the courage
to remove you from the
pedestal i placed you on.

you must have taken me for a fool
even if you did try to deny it.

but don't you know that
you never truly had a say in
how you would be immortalized

in all the lines i scrawl?

your entity was always mine to mould
with my choosing of
wrath
or beauty
the moment you got me alone.

how quickly you lost the privilege of the latter.

i've grown to enjoy pulling you apart
in every piece i write
in the same way you tore open all my scars
that you knew had yet to fully heal.

the words flow so easily,
and i know you read every single one.

so perhaps you're the fool
for how could you kiss a poet
and expect her to remain kind
after breaking her in the same way
you swore you never would?

i hope you like the way
i've immortalized your being;
after all,
my words are more honest
than you ever were.

on acceptance

my hands still shake
when i see your name
stomach caves in
at the sound of your voice
somehow familiar
yet foreign

(it's been so long
i was forgetting what
you sounded like
but i never asked
for a reminder)

there's one thing i discovered
each time i clawed at
the schema that is you
in attempt to rid myself
of what i already should have:

the more i fight you
the more you come back
the more stuck i become
in your quicksand

to fight you is to fall deeper
to securely anchor
my thoughts of you
and so i accept what is:

i can never shed you completely

i'll always react to
facets of you
because of the way
i once knew them

because you mattered

and i've come to know
that's okay

a glimpse of the rising sun

of lessons learned

but how could i ever hate you
when you taught my naïve heart
that it cannot force love
to grow between the cracks
in the curbs of old roads
between abandoned homes?

that when the sun sets
i should accept that it's time to go?

to stop watering the soil
in a barren land
that could not bear life
even if every rain
that has ever fallen
kissed the ground tonight?

loosen my lips
let the colour drain back into
knuckles strained
from tight grips on promises
of this love being
worth the wait.

darling, i still wait.

and so when the midnight whispers
smooth down my fiery hair
trace their new creed
"you deserve better"
on my icy arms
i can say that of course i do
i do
i do.

but i must give credit where it's due:
i learned it all from you.

on purpose

i want to be loved on purpose
want someone to look at me
just as how i gaze longingly at the moon
from my window each night
even after i've readjusted my glasses
and watch all the imperfections on her surface
come into focus

i want someone to choose me
like they do their favourite tea
to brew on a cold day,
for although it may burn sometimes
or not be sweet enough,
taste buds never forget the days
where a remedy to the hurt
was found in each sip

i want someone to call me
just to hear my voice at 3 pm
in the same way i always gravitate
towards my favourite songs
in a vast sea of melodies yet to be heard

and never grow tired of them
no matter how many days
they've been on repeat

i want someone who will reassure me;
i'm a companion that clings to you
while you're home
for i desire nothing more than your company
and i howl at the window while you're gone
out of fear that you won't return
because not everyone did
and i just need to be reminded
that you're different

i've been told that i'm a little too much;
i know that i'm a little too much
but if you don't mind,
if you want to be the first
to love me on purpose,
just know that i could give you the world
in all the spaces in-between

mangoes

when the mangoes stopped
tasting like you,
i knew it was time to remove
the dark mourning veil
and change into my sunday best.

the shackles had been broken,
setting me free into
a world of so many possibilities
of happiness
that i never could see
beyond your blockade.

i bite into ripe mangoes
let the juice drip onto
my white dress
until it looks like i've
harvested the sun.

and then, i dance.

and for the first time since
the mangoes stopped
tasting like you,
i don't mind
dancing alone.

red herring

to my red herring,

i don't think i've ever loved anyone as much as i loved
you.

cliche, isn't it?

it never occurred to me until i noticed how i look for you
in all the people i meet at crossroads who ask for entry into
my world. i agree on the condition that i can mould them
into as close an image of you as i can, but each
masterpiece crumbles before the clay dries.

i've never met anyone like you, and i don't think i ever
will.

sometimes i like to think about another life, one where i
like to think that we would have made it. we would stand
on stage and hold our interlaced fingers high above our
heads. the crowd would clap and cheer and scream,
"finally," while they throw thornless red roses at us. we'd
get our own place with 2 dogs and a big backyard that we
could transform into a garden to grow our own food. i

would have watched the skin around your honey eyes
slowly crease. you, my loosening curls lose their melanin.

we didn't get that chance, not in this life.

but at least we tried.

it's hard to swallow around the lump in my throat
reminding me that i barely know a time before you, and
sure as hell don't know a time after you (of course, there's
a first for everything) because for as long as it's mattered,
you were here: scooped me up with delicate hands from
my trenches; listened to every incoherent essay i'd
verbally compose as if there was a word count i needed to
meet; reassured me that my radiance was not too bright,
not for the right person. you'd always tell me that they just
weren't the right person.

who would have thought that you weren't either?

they wrote red herrings into our story. made all the clues
point to you until we hit the climax of the plot and i
realized i got it all wrong. i unintentionally chose the
ending to the book where the slow burn dwindles into
nothing, the charred pages crumbling into a heap. you

can't restore them when they're in black fragments that
turn to dust by your touch; i learned that the hard way. i
got lost in the memories, hooked on the need to have those
same things in the present.

but i'm accepting it for what it is, now.

i'm learning to let go.

though, don't be mistaken: you'll never be a stranger to
me.

the porch light will be on in case you ever want to stop by.

mundane love

they tell me that
after heartbreak,
that i should take time
to fall in love with myself again.

i know they mean well.

but i've always been a little too invested
in the stories of love in the movies;
i store all the fairy tale endings in a jar
and pick out plot lines each day
to live out in my head.

or, that's what i did until
i got a taste of the most mundane parts
of what it means to love someone.

i no longer crave extravagance
and well-written perfection
but rather the little things
that never get the attention.

i could bathe for hours in
the way it feels
that first moment you meet someone
and it all seems so right.

cooking with someone
in the rays of the sunrise
and accidentally set off
the smoke alarm
when the toast starts to burn.

the way we'll puff up our cheeks
as we try not to laugh at a joke
you made last week
when we're in a quiet room
with strangers.

when you reach for
my hand under the table
eating dinner as you meet my family
and all the stories i've told
begin to make sense.

my smile just a little contagious
from my place in the passenger seat

so you can't help but grin
through the force of the wind
from the rolled-down window.

bask in the proximity of your energy
find comfort in the prolonged silences
and just be.

it's the simple moments of the everyday that look most enticing as my fingers delicately search my mind's archives for stories to reminisce. they're the ones that bring comfort on the cold, gloomy days, and give that same feeling as the first sip of hot tea after the season's first snow: walking up and down aisles in the grocery store; recipes that ended in messes on my kitchen floor; falling asleep on your chest in the television's glow; the way you'd to tell stories but forget mid-way where they meant to go.

it was always the little things we did that painted the brightest smiles on my face, and they're the things i'll remember far longer than anything else.

- the stories don't hurt anymore

casiah cagan

morning

you draw shapes on my thigh to wake me
and help me rub
hallowed hollowness
from my tear ducts once i do

i want to crumble when i see
how the morning sun
makes your shy smile
glisten in millions of fragments
that illuminate the paint
peeling on the walls
(and my cautious heart)

we roll over on the mattress
and into august

you hold my face in your warm hands
as though it were the finest china
and i can't help but laugh
as the bed frame creaks
under the weight
of all we leave behind
in the rainy days of july

you say you'll make us
pancakes for breakfast
(blueberry, my favourite)
i say i'll try not to
take things so personally
(we both know i always will,
but you never seem to mind
reassuring me)

you kiss me softly
as you carry me to the kitchen—
you taste like hope—
and i let myself believe that
maybe i've found someone
good for me

how i know i've healed:

- the utterance of your name holds no weight. it does not sit on my chest and expel the air in my lungs, nor slash at my heartstrings until i bleed out in the night. the letters form a word like any other, an objective fact that simply exists. it is void of feeling.

- i can listen to the songs i once hastily skipped because i couldn't bear to face the thoughts of you that surfaced with each measure. i've fallen back in love with the melodies, the lyricism, the imagery, the careful crafting of each beat, strike, chord. they no longer remind me of what i used to try so hard to forget; there is nothing left to forget, and nothing left to remember.

- the persistence of relived memories and angry sobs that melted my pillowcase in the moonlight no longer ensue from the admittance that i sometimes miss the tenderness of our intertwined fingers. the moment passes as quickly as it comes; i don't dwell like i used to.

- my appetite has returned home from the place it vanished to. i don't pick at my food at the dinner table and pretend to not notice the raised eyebrows as my mother demands a list of the things i ate today.

- i finished watching *community* without you.

- i don't flinch when i see a car like the one you drive.

- i don't search for you in him.

acknowledgments

most people who know me know that i've been writing for as long as i can remember.

i was obsessed with writing short stories as a kid. whether they be about animals or mythical creatures or fictionalized twists of my own thoughts and fears, you could bet that i would be writing something (i especially loved the "and then i woke up" endings).

the first time i ever believed my writing might be good was in seventh grade. we had a short story assignment to complete, and naturally, i was excited.

i remember going to class one day, after submissions were due, and my teacher said that she really wanted to read one story to the class. i realized within the first few lines that it was mine. of course, once we pass the embarrassment that is a 12-year-old's slightly cringey and much-too-dark-for-her-age story, it felt good to not only be told that my work was well-written, but also see how gripping it was for my peers who, by the looks on their faces, were listening intently.

i thought, hey, maybe i *can* write.

i'm thankful for that.

i kept writing. short stories, songs, even poetry once i got to high school. it was fun. it was frustrating. nevertheless, i enjoyed it. but sharing my work got harder as years passed and i refrained from it for a long time. there's something so vulnerable in being able to share your work. it started to scare me. and i stopped writing creatively for a while. i stopped thinking i was good at it, or that i could write at all.

i maintained my writing hiatus into university, sticking mostly to academic writing. but i had a professor in my first year english class who changed that after a semester of both academic and creative assignments. i remember her making a comment on one of my final assignments telling me that i was a gifted writer; she said that she could see my work being published.

it gave me the best feeling, thus providing me with the
spark i needed to revisit my old work and get back into
writing. i took a creative writing class the next semester
and stayed in touch with that professor to meet and share
my ideas and get feedback on my writing. i'm convinced
that my writing improved exponentially that year, as did
my love of writing, and it truly is thanks to her. i'm forever
grateful for it.

i'm also grateful for my friends who have been so
encouraging of my writing, the ones who read everything i
write and make suggestions for topics to write about and
tell me that they enjoy everything i have to say. i don't
think that i remind them enough of how much i appreciate
their support.

when i'm ready to retreat into myself and give up on
writing out of fear that perhaps i've been lied to and i look
a little foolish with what i do, they remind me that even if i
do, so what? they've been my backbone and my saving
grace not only here, but in all other areas of my life too.
they're my cheerleaders in everything i do that make it
easier to get out of bed every day, especially on the days
when my heart is heavy and my mind is foggy and getting

out of bed seems like an impossible task. thank you for always having my back.

obligatory section thanking my family because, i can't complain, they've supported my writing since the very beginning when i was writing stories about dolphins and leprechauns. even though i sometimes hate being the designated grammar/spell-check/content police, i love that my passion for writing is taken seriously. it means the world to have a support system that starts right at home.

to anyone who has ever followed me or engaged with my content, even just once, writing comments and messages expressing how they feel seen and how strongly they connect to my words, thank you for reminding me why i do what i do. i like to tell myself that if i can make even one person feel something, it's worth it. i'm so thankful to have the privilege of a reach that is greater than a single person (though i admit that at times, it's terrifying to think that hundreds of people are reading my work).

and lastly, anyone who has inspired any of my pieces holds a particularly special place in my heart. i'm thankful for the opportunity to have had your life weave with mine in any capacity. whether i'm lucky to still have you around or

you have ventured on since passing through me, you've
taught me so much and made me feel so much in ways that
are indispensable. it feels fitting to end here with this quote
by uma thurman: "i still love the people i've loved, even if
i cross the street to avoid them.

about the author

casiah cagan is a writer who enjoys conjuring poetry on various topics, from current events to mental health, to love and heartbreak. on rare occasions, you may even get a short story out of her. when she isn't busy with school and work, you can find casiah baking vegan treats for her friends or re-watching *new girl* for the hundredth time. she currently holds a bachelor's degree in psychology and hopes to pursue a career somewhere at the intersection of school psychology and social justice. *a glimpse of the rising sun* is her first book.